Published Three Times a Month by THE RIDGWAY COMPANY

J. H. GANNON, President C. H. HOLMES, Secretary and Treasurer

Spring and Macdougal Streets · · New York, N. Y.
6, Henrietta St., Covent Garden, London, W. C., England

Entered as Second-Class Matter, October 1, 1910, at the Post-Office at New York, N. Y., under the Act of March 3, 1879. ARTHUR SULLIVANT HOFFMAN, Editor

Yearly Subscription, $6.00 in Advance Single Copy, Twenty-Five Cents

Foreign Postage, $3.00 additional. Canadian Postage, 90 cents.

Contents for July 30th, 1924, Issue

Occasionally one of our stories will be called an "Off-the-Trail" story, a warning that it is in some way different from the usual magazine stories, perhaps a little different, perhaps a good deal. It may violate a canon of literature or a custom of magazines, or merely be different from the type usually found in this magazine. The difference may lie in unusual theme, material, ending, or manner of telling. No question of relative merit is involved.

MAY
18th
1919

Adventure

PUBLISHED
TWICE A MONTH

BARONESS ORCZY
EUGENE P. LYLE, Jr
TALBOT MUNDY
GORDON YOUNG
J. ALLAN DUNN
CHARLES BEADLE

and others who tell
good stories well

Finish the Job!

5th LIBERTY
LOAN

Robert Kenneth Jones'

Starmont Pulp and Dime Novel Studies #4
ISSN 0885-0658

R. REGINALD
The Borgo Press
San Bernardino, California ▫ MCMXCII

Library of Congress Cataloging-in-Publication Data

Jones, Robert Kenneth
The lure of adventure / by Robert Kenneth Jones
p. cm. -- (Pulp & dime novel studies ; #4)
Includes Index.

1. Adventure stories, American--History and criticism. 2. Adventure stories--Periodicals--Publishing--United States--History--20th century. 3. Adventure (New York, N.Y.) I. Title. II. Series : Starmont pulp and dime novel studies ; no. 4.
PS374.A35J66 1989
813'.08709 -- dc20 89-34753
CIP

THE LURE OF ADVENTURE

Robert Kenneth Jones

In the twenties and thirties, if you wanted to journey to one of the four corners of the world, you didn't hop aboard a jet; you opened a pulp. Pulp magazines regularly stopped at far-flung ports of call, where adventurers hunted for pearls perhaps, or trekked through impenetrable forests to reach lost civilizations, or turned back the pages of history to view an exciting period of the past. Indeed, so little was known about many mysterious places on our globe, that whatever was said about them in magazines, books and the movies was readily accepted by an audience eager for vicarious thrills.

Who could resist the allure of a China of *femme fatales* like the Dragon Lady, the romance of a South Seas of sarong-clad seductresses like Dorothy Lamour, the excitement of a cattle drive ramrodded by a Hopalong Cassidy? In those days, the world was more idealized—and this aura tinged pulp writing, particularly that highlighted adventurous action in foreign lands.

Of the adventure-type pulps, many specialized. There were those chronicling the exploits of stalwart, soft-spoken but quick-shooting heroes and cattle-rustling desperadoes, intrepid captains of the clouds, crime-fighting Sherlocks and super heroes, to mention a few.

Far fewer were the general fiction pulps, covering a wide spectrum of adventures each issue. Of these, four, perhaps five, can be singled out as foremost among all such pulp magazines. They are Munsey's *Argosy*, McCall's *Blue Book*, Doubleday Doran's *Short Stories*, and The Ridgeway Company's (later Popular's) *Adventure*; there are many aficionados who class Street & Smith's *Popular* with them. In any case, all reflect high literary values in the writing that compare favorably not only with other pulps, but with just plain storytelling in any shape or form. For years, collectors have debated over which was the best—sometimes adding a few more titles, such as *All-Story* or *Everybody's*.

Let's end all conjecture. *Adventure* leads the rest, based on two aspects: quality writing and authenticity. Ron Goulart, in *Cheap Thrills*, notes that the magazine was "evenly divided between those who researched and imagined and those who had been there and recorded . . . either method was productive of effective adventure fiction."

The magazine prided itself on its commitment to telling it like it was—a stand that sometimes led to amusing, perchance heated, give-and-takes involving author and reader. Usually, the challenger, no matter how well informed, came out second best. Thus, when J. Allan Dunn's serial "Rovers Three" (Dec. 20, 1925) mentioned colors discernible in the dark, several readers took issue. Dunn rebutted that in tropic and semi-tropic latitudes in moonlight "color is distinguishable to a marked degree. Objects seem tinted perhaps but the degrees vary. The scarlet hibiscus will remain almost black, but the pinker blooms will be hued, so will the yellow plumaria petals, the purple of the bougainvillea, the orange of the native huapala trumpet-vine." Such little educational rejoinders were regularly supplied by authors apparently with all the facts at their fingertips.

A gun authority questioned Alan LeMay on his story, "Terlegraphy and the Bronc" (June 30, 1925). He liked it, but quibbled over taking the time to cock a gun, "when time meant life or death . . . and as everyone knows, cocking is unnecessary with a double-action revolver."

LeMay shot right back with, "I thought everyone knew that the stiff trigger action of an ordinary double-action gun spoils a man's aim. You get around that by cocking the hammer. You let the double-action rest until sometime you may want to empty the whole works pronto . . . . If you are in the habit, your thumb cocks that hammer as your hand draws.

And the thumb is quicker than the arm—don't let anyone tell you different . . . . Ask any old single-action man how long it took him to cock his gun, over and above the time it took to draw. A split second wasted? Bunk."

Such feisty answers not only reinforced the magazine's claim to authenticity, but added considerable spice to the "Camp Fire," the meeting place for readers, writers and editor. You were not only entertained, but educated too. "Camp Fire" was inaugurated in the June 1912 issue, a year and a half after the magazine started.

The first issue of *Adventure* was dated November 1910. For the next six years, the magazine appeared monthly, before going to two issues a month. This appreciation of *Adventure* covers the period 1915 (first issue in my collection) through 1925. It is rather detailed, since there is so much to comment on: personalities, stories, controversies—probably more than the average collector cares to know, but aspects that I personally wanted to give visibility to. In fact, a substantial report could be made on "Camp Fire" alone, so chock full of information, author comments and editorial peregrinations is it.

These early years are interesting ones to look at. During its monthly run, the magazine featured novels that really gave you something to bite into—sometimes totaling more than ninety pages. The editor had a lot to say about a lot of things, particularly the threat to our country from allowing so many foreigners to immigrate, the loss of our constitutional rights in a proposed gun control, and pacificism. He was a man of strong opinions.

Many of the outstanding writers who appeared in *Adventure* are heard from during this period—names like Talbot Mundy, W.C. Tuttle, Georges Surdez, William Byron Mowery, Gordon Young, Hugh Pendexter, Farnham Bishop, Arthur Gilchrist Brodeur, L. Patrick Greene, Arthur D. Howden Smith and H. Bedford-Jones. In addition, there were many other authors who, while gaining fame elsewhere, appeared in *Adventure* from time to time, such as Rafael Sabatini and

John Buchan.

While a study of the magazine during its entire history would seem worthwhile, it is felt that a close look at the first fifteen years will cover many of the high spots and provide a good understanding of what it was and where it was going.

In the early period, then, we find the long novel, a serial (two, when one was ending and another beginning) and perhaps six short stories, plus an occasional article or two, although the editor repeatedly stipulated that the magazine was for fiction, not fact. If there was no novel, there would be three novelettes, averaging about thirty to thirty-five pages each, within a 224-page format.

The poetry, while not notable, was easy to take: "Then here's to the plucky and happy-go-lucky, free-hearted, free-handed, amazingly candid, orating, debating, vivacious, sagacious, persistent, insistent, ostensible, sensible, rollicking, frolicking, itinerating and peregrinating, but nonhibernating, importunate, fortunate traveling-man," went one example.

The main impetus of the letters column then and throughout the magazine's colorful and long life, were the personal histories and anecdotes contributed by both authors and readers. Sometimes, contributors reported some noteworthy or exciting adventure, particularly during the World War I period. Other times, they would preface their remarks with something like, "Nothing much has happened in my life," and then go on to tell something interesting after all.

Typical of many such personal histories is this account by M.S. Wightman in the October 1915 issue. He explains how he drew on his experiences in the Philippines for his story, "An Occasional Hero." After graduating from Princeton in 1904, he went to the Philippines as secretary to the vice governor, where he stayed for seven years, then summered on a ranch in Montana and camped out in the Rockies. ". . . although I do not consider myself more than a fair horseman, I could actually outride and outmanage a goodly number of the men on the ranch. . ."

One time he stood face to face with death, he says, while a

guest on a submarine in Manila Bay. The main tank was open, when suddenly, the sub plunged downward. "Why the main tank did not give way, drowning us out of hand, only the god of strains knows." The commander calmly ordered the closing of the tank's valve, and all were saved. Many such personal histories were rather mild. But they have retained an interest and flavor even after all these years.

In the same issue, the editor notes: "The following word from an American at the front, with the French Foreign Legion, was so exceptionally interesting that our older brother *Everybody*'s publishes it in its current issue. But that is no reason why all of the "Camp Fire" should not also hear what one of has to say." The soldier explains how he found a January 1915 copy of *Adventure* in the village of Craonne, retaken by the French from the Germans. Some of his comments about the war are worth hearing at this time.

"The high-power rifle is a joke. I have seen for the last 10 months continual firing from one trench to another, sometimes at distances of 50 to 75 meters. I have seen uncalled-for panics take both sides, on a dark night when each trench would be a continual line of fire, hundreds of men firing hundreds of cartridges each and I have never seen a man killed by a rifle ball.

"But if you want to see a shambles, visit a trench just after a few hand grenades have been thrown into it. The great sport here on both sides is hand-grenading the other fellow. How played? Well, you leave your trench on a dark night with three or four grenades . . . No crawling on hands and knees goes—too dangerous . . . I have taken over three hours to cover a hundred yards. Arrived at the other trench you keep still until you hear the relief coming, generally between 11 and 12, or between one and two . . . you jump up, throw your grenade and run as if the monster of Sleepy Hollow were after you."

That December (1915) appeared an 89-page novel by Harold Kellock and George Schuyler Schaeffer, hardly household names, even in *Adventure*. It's about an engineer driving a railroad through a Latin-American republic during a revolution, and it crackles with vitality. The contents page promises: "Before you've read far you'll want to rip off your coat and help him." The protagonist is a dynamic man, a couple of years under forty, who perseveres against heavy odds and wins a young lady to boot.

As if this wasn't enough woman interest in a man's-oriented magazine, the cover highlights Patrick and Terence Casey's "The Story of William Hyde," as "one of the greater romantic stories of action ever written." This was a period during which *Adventure* allowed love interest in its stories, a policy that would soon change. The latter example, incidentally, reflecting the lost race theme fantasy authors were so fond of, felt uncomfortable in the reading. It is begun in the first person by a young ship oiler, who meets Hyde and hears his story, also told in the first person. So you have a four-part serial in first person second-hand, so to speak.

It was during this "romantic" period that the northwoods courtships of Robert and Kathrene Pinkerton took place. There is something very appealing about adventures taking place in the snow-wrapped northlands, where the Mounted Police fight temperatures 20 to 30 below zero to bring in their man, where a young explorer or trapper bests the trackless wastes to win wealth and the woman, where danger lurks around the bend of the trail, and fur company fights fur company for the right to immense fortunes.

In a way, these stories set in the frozen wilderness bear a close affinity to tales of the old West. In these situations of comparative primitiveness, where an inhospitable environment brings out the best or worst of a person, the triumph of good over evil is an uncomplicated and satisfying resolution. Northwoods romances in this time vied with westerns for reader appeal. Such a magazine as *Short Stories* continued to feature a story in each issue set in a northwoods locale for more than 30 years, although *Adventure* phased them out in the early twenties, and carried them sporadically thereafter.

Writing from their own small cabin, snow-bound half the

year, the Pinkertons speak glowingly of the north, somewhat in the glorifying manner of James Oliver Curwood, although without his excessive love interest. One of their stories starts in this fashion: "No one could escape the first sense of awe that was engendered by the spectacle. . . . From Wallace's seat he could see the great stretch of water with its distant shore. It lay there quietly, seemingly immovable, and yet always it pushed and forced itself out and down to crash and boil upon the rocks so far below. That expanse of lake behind that great drop for which it seemed to wait so patiently, gave to the waterfall a background of reserve force, of invincibility, of permanence, which no single stream, rushing through a narrow gorge to tumble with greater volume from a greater height, could possibly possess."

Often, the north is inimitable. "The wind scattered and whirled the flames of their small fire, blowing smoke into their faces, carrying all the heat away from them. It strangled and it burned, it roared and it moaned and it shrieked, it brought its message of terror as well as its physical suffering, and in time, a depressing effect which added to their struggle to live."

The hardy souls inhabiting this inhospitable land are as resilient and unspoiled as the wilderness that nurtures them. "Twilight Jack . . . lived in the wilderness because he loved it. He understood it, knew when to humor it, when to affront it. . . . The forest was his mistress. . . . Those who come out of the wilderness are great, strong men, greater in spirit than in strength, stronger in mind than in body. And yet, so strange is the wilderness, they come out chastened despite their defiance, softened despite the rigors of their lives."

Such rhapsodic panegyrics are not unusual. Most of the writers who set their stories in this land showed a genuine love for it which communicates itself to the reader. In this respect, the Pinkertons bore a close affinity to writers who came before, and followed, writers such as Curwood, James B. Hendryx, William Byron Mowery and Rex Beach.

In "The Trail of the Black Fox" (Jan. 3, 1918), the Pinkertons present an unusual northwoods adventure, a detective story that actually makes use of investigative procedures instead of the usual broad approaches other authors employ, such as matching a moccasined footprint to someone and then trailing him into the cold fastness to capture him. Twilight Jack is introduced and unravels by deduction the murder at a fox farm in the Canadian wilds. The love interest involves an ethnologist and the daughter of the owner of the farm.

Twilight Jack returns to solve another murder, in a later issue. In the 1918-19 period, the Pinkertons wrote three stories about the three friends, Tom Gill, Marshall Wells and Jimmy Dunn, and Jimmy Dunn Wells, named after Wells' friend, and their adventures in an inaccessible area known as the barren grounds, where they are beset by renegade Chippewyan Indians. Their last story together in *Adventure* appeared March 18, 1920. Robert continued alone, in *Short Stories*. The northwoods romance was continued awhile in the magazine by Samuel Alexander White, who wrote several short stories about the rivalries between various fur companies.

The issues during World War I often contained a sad note, announcing the death of an author who had appeared in the pages, a member of what the editor referred to as the Writers' Brigade. The October 18, 1917 issue contains a letter from William Hope Hodgson, who died in Flanders April 17 the following year. "Lord man! You'd like to be out here to see and hear some of the sights and sounds of war. I've heard the machine-gun fire rise into an absolute scream of sound, by hundreds, a devilish torment of shrill, abominable noise, impossible to imagine in the mass. And then again, at other times, I've heard a lonely gun in some unseen field at night tap-tapping its disconsolate death-message across some stretch of darkness."

A few days before his death, he had survived a dangerous assignment as observation officer of his brigade. His wife sent a clipping to the editor which was partly reprinted. "The enemy had broken through right up to the guns . . . the commanding officer, Lieutenant Hodgson, another officer and a few NCOs fought a rear-guard action across three miles of country amid a hail of machine-gun and rifle fire, hotly pursued by the enemy. Lieutenant Hodgson climbed to the roof of a wrecked farmhouse as F.O.O. under very heavy shell and rifle fire. All of that gallant little band got away, but with the loss of all their kit, even their Sam Browne belts and their revolvers."

Feelings ran high during the war. One anonymous reader complained that the magazine would not be successful with the likes of such an author as Hapsburg Liebe. Liebe himself answer in "Camp-Fire," noting that there was almost no German blood in him, that his people came from Holland and settled in Virginia a long time ago, that his father was three-fourths English, his mother Scotch-Irish-English, and he himself a "lanky, squirrel-killing, banjo-playing, fiddling, hound dog-loving Tennessee mountaineer. . ."

The editor, Arthur Sullivant Hoffman, was quick to castigate individuals who assumed someone was something he wasn't. But that didn't stop Hoffman from striking out at anyone in the country with "Teuton written all over him," mixing with us and "reading a newspaper printed in the language of our German enemies," as he did in another issue. A few years later he came back with, "This country is rotten with pro-British, pro-Irish and pro scores of other nations. If I could, I'd wipe out all of it, lock, stock and barrel. The only kind of propaganda we need in this country is pro-American. . ." (August 30, 1922).

Hoffman was somewhat of a paradox: a man who time after time expressed a great tolerance for others' opinions, who reflected a resolute honesty, and took a judicious approach on many subjects, only to shriek imprecations at the United States' immigration policy of allowing so many foreigners to come into the country and pollute its national strain, and pound his chest on several other issues. He criticized the National Guard as an inefficient operation, and grew positively choleric at the thoughts of gun control—an insidious threat to our constitutional rights.

Hoffman had served under Turnbull White, *Adventure*'s first editor, for about a year or so before becoming editor himself, when White went to *Everybody's*. He held the helm in a firm hand, expressing his opinions regularly in "Camp-Fire," writing voluminously, both to authors and readers, and devising various departments for the magazine. "Ask Adventure," the meeting place information section answering questions from readers on a variety of subjects, began in the February 1917 issue. The January issue announced the free service: "When I look back over the years I am amazed at the multiplicty and variety of the occasions on which we have been called into the personal and private affairs of our readers and writers to be of what service we could. . . . Marriage, divorce, broken engagements, deaths, funerals, hospitals, inheritances, in all these and a thousand other problems . . . have we been asked to take a hand at one time or another." Within a year, such questions as, "Is it possible for a young chap to learn prospecting from a good correspondence school?" to, "I desire information on the New Zealand rabbit," were appearing in "Ask Adventure." Several of *Adventure*'s authors conducted the Q&A department: Capt. A.E. Dingle (just Captain Dingle on his story byline), who single-handedly sailed a sloop from New York to Bermuda, at that time a modern-day feat. He covered the Indian and Atlantic oceans; Raymond S. Spears on the eastern U.S.; Hapsburg Liebe, the same area; Edgar Young, South America; Gordon MacCreagh, Asia; George E. Holt, Africa; Charles Beadle, Africa.

That year Hoffman also began "Lost Trails," the meeting place where readers could ask for help on the whereabouts of friends and acquaintances. A very popular feature and one that brought the readers closer together than any other publication could ever boast, was the establishment and subsequent listing of "Camp-Fire" stations. The editor broached the idea in the August 3, 1919 issue, that of setting up local headquarters around the country, where people could pick up mail, leave word for someone, or just meet kindred spirits. As he explained, it could be a place of business or simply a telephone number, or someone's home. The idea quickly grew, after a tentative start. By mid-1920 there were 27 "Camp-Fire" stations, in California, District of Columbia, Washington, Oregon, Philippine Islands and Canada. Within five years, they were worldwide and numbered in the hundreds, from Egypt to England, Canada to Cuba, Australia to Belgium, and most U.S. states in between. Readers often wrote in to report on meeting new friends through these stations. Another unifying force were the "Camp-Fire" buttons proudly worn by readers. In 1924, one reader gave the startling information that while he was in the Canal Zone, "every fifth man wore your "Camp-Fire" button. Seems like I'm putting it a little strong, but it's only the truth."

Hoffman was a man of indefatigable energies. In 1914, he spearheaded an American Legion, which drew the endorsement of Theodore Roosevelt and Maj. Gen. Leonard Wood. It was in keeping with his fierce desire for America to be prepared, a subject he often expounded in "Camp-Fire." As director, he allowed the name to be used by the veterans of World War I, and thus can be considered the founder of our present-day Legion.

There were many "big names" among authors in the early years of *Adventure*. Talbot Mundy, whose stories in a pulp assure it of a high price among collectors, much as a Burroughs' story does, sold his first story to the magazine in 1911. He would continue to appear there for the next 29 years. H. Rider Haggard gave his followers another Allan Quatermain epic, a serial beginning in the January 1917 issue ("Finished"), the third of the trilogy including "Marie" and "Child of Storm." This was one of the few times the magazine reprinted from a book.

Another exception was Rafael Sabatini's "The Sea Hawk." The author had appeared in the *Adventure* with the first publication of "Captain Blood" years earlier. Then his Brethren of the Main series—short tales of Captain Blood—was seen in several issues in 1921. A year later, *The Sea Hawk* was reprinted, in five installments. The editor explained how he had read the book and been so fascinated by it, he decided to print it as an experiment, since magazines ordinarily did not follow that procedure, and he feared it could mean a loss of prestige. The readers justified his selection and voted the story in first place for that year. Sabatini took a bow in 1923 with two true life adventures from "Historical Entertainment Nights," of Casanova and Sir Walter Raleigh. These appeared before book publication this time.

For years readers voted on the best stories of the year, a practice that ended shortly after the twenties started. For the last several years, three or four names repeatedly topped the list. As might be expected, one was Talbot Mundy, as popular today among collectors as he was among readers then.

Another was Arthur O. Friel, who explored in the steaming jungles of the Orinoco that winds through Venezuela, an area he knew first hand. A third was Gordon Young. A prolific author, whereas a Friel would produce a serial in three installments, a Young would come up with five or six.

Among his heroes was Hurricane Williams, and Don Everhard, known as the two-gun fighter with the poker face, both of whom appeared in many stories. The difficulty with these early Young stories seems to be in their wordiness. Everhard closed with Gaboreau in "Baboreau the Terrible" (November 1, 1918) and they meet again in "From Behind Masks," this time a short serial in two parts (May 18, 1919). An example of Young's turgidity is seen in the following: "Among the minor influences that contributed to my resolution to do whatever could be done toward finding the person or persons who seemed as elusive, as impalpable, as shadows in the night, was the fact that Gowar McFarland had been among the few of our numerous family that stood up for me, avowed a liking for me, sought my company."

Told in the first person, it reflects a pretentious approach. "I am afraid of many things, but the dark is not one of them. Moreover, I was not unarmed, and in the matter of exchanging shots I have no reason to feel nervous, no matter who the other person may be. If this sounds much like boasting, I can only reply that, more times than not, I can hit a small coin flipped in the air at 10 paces."

To belabor a point, here is an example of ludicrous back-and-forth between Everhard and the villain.

"'What is your game? I don't like to work blind—'

"'What's that?'

"'I'll do any work, but I don't want to work blind . . . I'll make good money working alone.'

"'You try to work alone, and I'll have you killed . . .'

"'That's all right. But what is the big idea? I'll take chances, but I don't work with a light.'

"'Without a what?'

"'A light—something that shows where I am going—what I am doing.'

"'You won't do as I direct?'

"The question he asked was a threat."

Well, finally you can figure out who was speaking. But the whole routine sounds like a parody, and is particularly dated by today's standards.

Young told an exciting story, but padded it unmercifully. It's interesting to compare these early efforts with some of his later stories, particularly the western chronicles about Red Clark, the man who never told a lie. Some appeared in *Adventure* in the thirties, and many others were printed in *Short Stories*, which seemed to have attracted quite a few authors who established a name for themselves earlier in *Adventure*, such as Captain Dingle, William Byron Mowery, H. Bedford-Jones, L. Patrick Greene, W.C. Tuttle, James B. Hendryx and Ernest Haycox.

These later efforts by Young were models of economy, of terse description and mounting melodrama. Red Clark, the hero of many such stories, first appeared in Young's "La Rue of the 88," a five-parter that started in the December 30, 1925 issue of *Adventure*. He plays a secondary role in that one, but exhibits the same uncompromising honesty that became his trademark later, when he was the featured performer. In any case, these early Young efforts found favor with the British critics, who likened Young to Joseph Conrad, and of course, with the magazine readers. As might be surmised, the western was one of the staples of the magazine. This was true of several other types of stories too, such as frontier tales (mainly chronicled by Hugh Pendexter), adventures at sea, the far north, of course, in early issues, jungle explorations (frequently narrated by Greene and Friel), and Norse sagas (as exemplified by Arthur D. Howden Smith). I'm speaking here of the period under consideration, only to the end of 1925. It is surprising, in view of the wide interest in Custer, and the many letters reporting on various aspects of the massacre that the magazine received for years and years, that cavalry stories were not printed. But in any case, one of the continuing favorites was the western.

Ah, the western. Just what is its appeal? Who would think that a person today, used to so many modern conveniences, and about as unlikely to fight at the drop of a hat as a prairie dog, would respond so resoundingly to this period of early Americana.

Really, now, who in his right mind would want to live in a cowtown, where the streets are so dusty in dry weather you can't see across, and so mucky in wet weather you can't get across; where the only decoration is a calico dress worn by a woman; where the false fronts of the stores present a drab, unrelieved grimy-windowed, pock-marked, unpainted and deteriorating view unrelieved by the flat, sun-baked sage brush and alkali, unfit for man nor beast; and where the main amusement is clumping into a saloon to get drunk, spit on the floor, lose a few dollars at the faro table, and stagger back to the ranch for a hard day of bulldozing and cowpunching the next day? Not to mention the ever-present danger from rowdy, undisciplined and quick-on-the-trigger bullies who infested every town.

Well, there may be some exaggeration here, but not much. And yet, this particular period of American history—and for the most part, this encompasses those few years taking place after the Civil War, into the nineties—lives today (whether realistically or not) in book after book, story after story, tirelessly recreating the bloody Indian fighting, the struggle to establish a homestead, the long cattle drives, a lone marshal's heroic efforts to bring law and order to his town—all the many difficulties and dangers, now viewed romantically, of carving civilization out of a wilderness.

One of the main reasons for its appeal is, perhaps, as already noted, the depiction of life at its most elemental level, stripped of pretension and sophistication. Maybe as we get older, we respond more readily to the western's unwritten code that good always triumphs over bad. In the western, it is always black and white; there's no doubt who the good guys are. That's a tiresome tradition, but one that has appeal, nevertheless.

Contributing his part to it, William Patterson White wrote several serials and novels in the easy, colloquial fashion that characterized the western of those days. Indeed, western fiction then is as far from today's fare, much of it sex-tinged, as William S. Hart's "Gun Fighter" of the movies is from Gene Wilder's "Blazing Saddles." William Patterson, not to be confused with Samuel Alexander mentioned earlier, thus keeps the action moving in this fashion ("Heart of the Range," five-part serial, February 3, 1921): "'You've said yore li'l piece,' (Racey Dawson, the hero talking) 'and for a feller who was belly-achin' so loud about keepin' out of this deal it strikes me yo're a-gettin' in good an' deep—buyin' up mortgages an' all.'" His serial "Lynch Lawyers" topped the readers' poll for 1919.

Several other western writers penned stories during this time, but the most frequently appearing and enjoyable of them all is W.C. Tuttle, or Tut, as he signed his letters. In the teens he specialized in outrageous humor, involving several of his pet characters, like Magpie Simpkins, Ike Harper, Dirty Shirt Jones, Henry Peck, Telescope Tolliver, residents of such prepossessing place as Blue Nose and Piperock.

His stories then were written often in the first person, present tense with "sez" for says, "jist" for just, etc., and in a vernacular that was hard to read. Because of his humor, some readers questioned the "west" he depicted. The editor snapped back with the fact that Tuttle had never been east of Montana. More about Tuttle surfaces in other issues. We learn that his father was appointed sheriff of Dawson County, Montana, when the other sheriff was hiding from the vigilantes. Many of Tut's characters were drawn from real life, he notes. By 1921, he had forsworn the humor-only type story, except for the infrequent reappearance, in favor of an easy-going, action-western. This is when he hit his stride. His new heroes were not the travesties of the earlier incarnations, but combined ludicrousness with derring-do. His Skeeter Bill, the horse thief who won't lie, is a crane-like, long-legged, skinny-handed, solemn individual. Both he and Brick Davidson, another Tut hero, are nonchalant, easy-going individuals, probably somewhat in the cast of the author himself. Thus Brick, in "Sun Dog Trails" (July 3, 1921): "'Gotta, eh? Why didn't yuh go to a school where they teaches yuh to talk with your mouth?'" And the insouciant Skeeter Bill (March 30, 1922): "'You shot Jeff Billings?'

"Skeeter nodded indifferently.

"'Why? . . .'

"'Billings lied.' . . .

"'You killed him because he lied?'

"'Uh-huh,' indifferently . . .

"'What did he lie about, Sarg?'

"'You ought to know,' meaningfully. 'You told him what to say, Leeds,'"

As can be seen, Tuttle certainly didn't forsake the light touch that produces a smile if not a laugh when he began his new type of story. How's this for an opening?

"It was a hot day in Marlin City, the country seat of Sun-Dog County. It has often been said that there was only one tree between Marlin City and the Arctic Circle to break the north winds of winter, and that the aforementioned tree was too far north to afford Marlin City any shade during the summer." ("Tangled Trails," May 20, 1922).

Although Brick and Skeeter Bill appeared several times, it was Hashknife Hartley who captured reader favor. He was a tall, laconic cowboy, typical of Tuttle's more or less average-type western hero, who rode in and out of many mysteries during this time. Hashknife was seen in *Adventure* as early as 1917, but the narratives were in the somewhat bumptious first-person style Tuttle then employed, in this case told by his sidekick, Sleepy Stevens. The later accounts in the third person, are fun to read and somewhat addictive, although predictive. Tuttle has a lot of fun with names. Every story is crowded with colorful cognomens, usually alliterative: Peppermint Poole, Musical Matthews, Liniment Lucas, Tombstone Todd, Forty Dollar Dion, Swan River Smith. An occasional Buck or Tex may appear, but sound unimaginative and out of place.

The solemn-visaged Hashknife is a fatalist, but not above forcing an issue, and is handy with both gun and fist. He and Sleepy are always searching for the ideal place to settle in and raise cattle. But even when they seem to have found it, that is after Hashknife solves a murder or two and restores law and order, the two drifters move on. They speak disparagingly of getting involved, and then proceed to do so. They function somewhat in the manner of a Sherlock Holmes and Dr. Watson, with Hashknife sifting clues, making discoveries, but keeping things to himself until a propitious moment, as for instance, a trial. Then he unmasks the villains and usually shoots two or three himself to save the situation. He and Sleepy are rated top hands, so they never have trouble finding work, when they lope into town. Through good standing in the Cattlemen's Association, Hashknife is quickly accepted. None of this "misunderstood hero" business for Tut. Tuttle continued writing the Hashknife stories into the forties.

After many experiences as a trapper and hunter, a miner, salesman, semipro baseball player, cartoonist, bookkeeper and finally fiction writer for *Adventure*, Tuttle moved to Hollywood in 1918—a change of locale that undoubtedly helped him in selling Universal on the idea of filming some of his stories. The movie company made more than 20 shorts about Magpie and Dirty Shirt and the Piperock hoi poloi. Several of his novels in *Adventure* were published by book companies.

The Hashknife stories, while contemporary westerns, read like an earlier period, with the only reference to modern times mention of the movies. Just about all of the other westerns by other authors were set in the old west. An exception, though, was Jackson Gregory's serial, "Man to Man" (December 18, 1919), and the result is very pleasing, with the hero, Steve Packard, clashing with hot-tempered Terry Temple. In fact, it is just this male-female give-and-take, mild romance, but nevertheless an area the magazine was shunning, that makes for a provocative account. Here is one typical encounter:

"'You stand aside or I'll run you down!"

"With no intention of going under the wheels, Steve waited until the last moment and then jumped. But not to the side as Terry had anticipated. Obeying his impulse and taking his chance, he sprang up on her running board . . .

"'We meet again,' he laughed sociably. 'Howdy!'

"Her lips tight pressed, she gave her attention for a moment to her wheel and the rutty road in front of her. Her cheeks were red and grew redder. Perhaps a dozen men here and there upon the street had seen. She had meant them to see; it would have tickled her not a little to have had them note Steve Packard flying wildly to the side of the road while she shot by."

Norman-occupied Sicily in the 12th century is the setting Farnham Bishop and Arthur Gilchrist Brodeur used in a series about the Lady Fulvia. It seems some robber baron or other was always after this fair daughter of Arnulfo for her beauty, but especially her lands. She outwits Gaimar the Grim (May 18, 1918), and turns the tables on the brutal, superstitious brothers, Odo and Sigismundo (June 3, 1918). She returns in a novel (mid-February 1920) to face the dreaded Mahdi. Her father has died, and she alone rules Rocca Forte, "the key to the casket which held Palermo, the jewel of "Sicily," that tho powerful barons covet. Ian Dhu Mackay, from the Scot highlands, stands with Fulvia against the Mahdi, the fanatic heretic Moslem sect. This is a marvelous romance, when intrigue and quick death lurk everywhere, when faction allies with faction to forward devious plots, and when swords leap into play at the drop of an eyebrow. Fulvia, proud and disdainful of all who woo her, is determined she won't succumb to Ian, but . . .

Brodeur and Gilchrist wrote jointly and separately, bringing authenticity to their stories, no matter in what period set. As was typical of nearly every *Adventure* author then, they put considerable research into their stories. Professor Brodeur, of the University of California, thus explains the situation in Sicily at the time of the story. King Roger fought the German emperor, who invaded Italy. Sicily was not directly under the gun, thanks to Roger's wily manipulations, most specifically his wooing of the Moslems, descendants of the Arab conquerors his father and uncle had overthrown. This angered the church, and the Pope denounced him for not joining in the second Crusade (1147-9). The Mahdi were Mohammedans who declared against worship of the saints and of the attributes of Allah, Brodeur tells his readers.

Bishop alone wrote about Yankee privateers of the 18th century, while Brodeur in his solo efforts devoted two series to swordsmen of fortune in the 12th century. Interestingly enough, one of his characters appears in a substantial role in a story about the other, and reference is made to events that brought the two together earlier.

Then later, Brodeur writes a series about this individual and recounts those particular events. The first series is about Pierre Faidit, in the service of Count Alphonse-Jourdain of Toulouse. He meets Alienor, wife of King Louis of France, who murders Alphonse, and this *femme fatale* plies her wily machinations in the second series, too, about the troubadour-swordsman Cercaman, in the service of Count Raymond-Berenger of Barcelona. Like "The Hand of the Mahdi," swords fly and blood runs in these stories.

About this time, that is 1921-22, Brodeur complained to the editor at the edict against woman-interest in the stories. He pointed out that in the periods in which his stories were set there was much womanizing, and the people lived lusty lives, which he had been forced to ignore. The argument got nowhere; Hoffman countered by citing the overwhelming reader demand for fiction without any love angles to it. Of course, the pulps always proved wary of such entanglements, but many did indeed emphasize the love element (as long as it led to marriage). It's too bad that *Adventure*, which prided itself on its authenticity, should play down such an important aspect in its stories.

As noted, sea stories were seen regularly in the magazine. Arthur D. Howden Smith, very shrewd in devising a series that could carry him along for many appearances, wrote about Captain McConaughy, a bluff Cornish woman hater, who nevertheless has a soft spot for Miss Tabitha McNish, the managing director of the Red Funnel Line for whom he sails. The stories involve not his feelings for his employer, but rather his blustery and forceful methods of saving the shipping line always in the nick of time.

A longer lasting series is John Webb's, about One-Two Mac. The first one appears in the August 10, 1923 issue. Capt. James McGuire, of the *Hawk*, which ranges the Caribbean delivering cargo, is hated by his crew for his tyrannical ways, yet defended by them every time there is a crisis. This love-hate anomaly heightens the mystique of the captain's character: that of a short, middle-aged man with a dour personality, whose fists can floor bullies twice his size. The stories are written in an ingratiating way, with One-Two Mac sometimes to the fore, and at other times, a sort of background benevolence whose presence straightens things out.

Like so many other authors, Webb notes that One-Two Mac was drawn from life, after a master of a Central

American passenger ship on which Webb was second mate. And he, too, like so many others, is called upon to defend his position. A reader assails him for statements in one of his stories about hungry soldiers during the way. The reader says he was with the Nutrition Corps, and Webb should not write so "keerless like." Webb served as bosun and replied that he spent six months in France, and talked with all kinds of soldiers. He noted that the food aboard ship was unfit for a dog, and the Army food was even worse.

Although the editor occasionally affirmed that there was really no place in the magazine for fact articles, he continued to use them almost on a regular basis. In fact, every issue included a vignette or two on aspects of early history in our country, and often long accounts about individuals and events.

One of the favorites for the shorter presentations was Uncle Frank Huston, a Civil War veteran. Often, the editor would send someone's letter to the magazine to Uncle Frank to answer. He was somewhat of a testy nature, but Hoffman thought highly of him, and spoke thusly: "Camp-Fire" is sure the place for differences of opinion, but—well, words have a trick of appearing a bit harder on paper than they're meant. We're all friends together and we'll all have to watch so that our words will sound as friendly from the printed page as if we could all talk together personally. Now and then Uncle Frank Huston lets go with a wallop, but we all have known him and liked him for a long time, he's old enough to be a daddy to most of us and, well, he's Uncle Frank and that's enough."

One series of fact articles was very unusual, in that it was written by a full-blooded Zulu, who had learned English and thus gave first-hand accounts of life in his village—a refreshing change from the usual background derived from text books. Santie Sabalala's vivid pictures of savage life include one about a woman believed to be a witch (December 20, 1921). The villagers tie her to a limb of a tree, with a heavy stone on her right wrist, forcing it down. After two days, they cut off her arm at the shoulder. "They picked her up and walked over to the gate, slipping often with the mud and water under their feet. Arrived there the warriors gave the body a big swing and let go. The body sailed in the air, then fell with a splash in the rushing waters. It floated for a time, disappeared, then appeared and then was lost to sight for all time, as both log and woman were carried by the water down a hill that had become a waterfall." And all this caused by a little boy supposedly bewitched. But before we censure such primitive practices, it should be remembered that in Puritan New England women were sometimes burned at the stake when a child complained he was made sick by the evil eye.

For years, readers had been commenting, arguing and speculating in "Camp-Fire" on such subjects as how dangerous the bite of a tarantula was, whether there was such a critter as a hoopsnake, able to grab its tail in its mouth and roll down hills, how to shoot an arrow, how to train a horse to saddle, whether Wild Bill Hickok was really a hero; and the never-ending controversy over striking someone with the barrel of a pistol, not the butt.

One favorite subject was cow-milking snakes, with one expert averring that the snake's fangs would prevent this feat. However, Santie Sabalala offers an eye-witness account in his "In Kaffir Kraals" series that has to be one of nature's strange manifestations. He notes (April 30, 1922) that as a young boy he saw a huge snake hanging to a low branch of a tree by its tail, that "had wrapped itself around the cow's back and forward of the udders in such a way that they, the udders, would be under compression and leak. It had turned the upper part of its body around the hind legs and inserted itself between the legs—and with the side of its mouth was drinking the milk as it streamed out of the teats."

Africa was the setting for L. Patrick Greene's stories about The Major, whose "smooth, round, clean-shaven face wore an almost vacuous look, an impression that was strengthened by the monocle which he wore in his right eye." The first appearance was November 1, 1919. The action takes place in the Transvaal, where The Major is accompanied by his Hottentot servant, Jim. Beneath his foppish exterior, The Major (never named) is a steady, cool and keen individual who rights wrongs, and at the same time amasses a fortune in diamonds. At one point, he admits he has lost the money he made, and that he wants to end his outlaw existence and return to civilization. But like Hashknife and Sleepy, he never attains his avowed desire. The Major later continued his exploits in *Short Stories*, popular enough there to rate several covers. For a period, Greene worked on the staff of *Adventure* and was not allowed to write for it; when he returned to free-lancing full time, he once again took up abode in Africa.

Among his later stories, that is during 1925, were several set in Rhodesia, and concerned with a wise Jewish trader named Isaacs and Miles, the missionary, who tries to superimpose his religious beliefs on the natives. Miles slowly learns to accept their ways of doing things, under the patient and often humorous tutelage of Isaacs, at the same time both men face various threats to the status quo in unscrupulous individuals wishing to exploit the territory.

Another author who was fascinated with Africa was Georges Surdez. His first story in *Adventure* was "The Yellow Streak" (October 10, 1922), and soon he was in full swing with the Foreign Legion. Although French was his mother tongue, Surdez wrote in English. His style is reminiscent of de Maupassant's, with its effortless transitions between visual descriptions and actions. In construction it reminds one of the earlier Frenchman, and reflects a Gallic charm typical of so many French authors. In fact, Surdez may be the most artistic of *Adventure*'s many contributors. He could move from one viewpoint to another, from one tense to another, and backward and forward in time so smoothly that those manipulations which often exasperate the reader fall into place so naturally they are almost unnoticed.

"Outside the Walls" (May 30, 1923) exemplifies Surdez' best traits. Initially, it focuses on the commander of a military unit in a Sahara town, shows his character with an economy of description, then switches to a private who struck a sergeant and is punished by being sent to an outpost of criminals to do manual labor. There is an Arab rebellion, and a lot of touch-and-go excitement. Here the author goes from the past to the present tense, from third person to second with no loss of forward project and interest. He understood the appeal of contrasting emotions: "One of the little soldiers, sensing his helplessness, wept, the tears rolling down his beardless cheeks, but his teeth were set, his bayonet ready."

When Surdez wrote of the horrors of military penitentiaries in North Africa in one of his stories, a reader inquired if conditions were actually as bad as depicted. Surdez replied that they were worse. He noted that an NCO in charge of a camp in Morocco left his prisoners without water for several days, then gave them some so salted as to be undrinkable. A French journalist had visited the camps in Morocco, Algeria and Tunis, and written a series of articles, which Surdez used as a basis for some of his stories. The author would visit Northern Africa on occasion, and remained in touch with both natives there and French officials, which lent a verisimilitude to his presentations.

It's not clear if the first Surdez story to be printed first appeared in *Adventure* or if his first story for *Adventure* was "The Yellow Streak." Similarly, many other authors rose and took a bow, as the editor put it, on the occasion of their first story, if not first of all at least first in the magazine.

Thus we meet Harold A. Lamb, who did all his research in the library at Columbia University, Goulart notes, in the October 1, 1917 issue. He writes there on Sir Francis Drake, and later would turn his talent exclusively to the 16th and 17th centuries and the barbaric adventures of Khlit the Cossack and Abdul Dost, a Mongol.

Lamb became an authority on Mongol history, and his later biography of Genghis Khan would be the first authentic one published in this country, and apparently the second in the English language.

Earlier that year James B. Hendryx had his first story, not

about the north he specialized in later, but about a Tennessee feud transplanted to New York City. In this case, as sometimes happened, Hoffman mixed up the author's letter and story, so Hendryx' brief biography appears with a later story. Born in Sauk Center, Minnesota, Hendryx worked for a railroad, punched cows, worked in Alaska and then settled down to magazine and newspaper work. As a youngster, he chummed with Sinclair Lewis' older brother, and Sinclair Lewis himself went on to work briefly for the magazine. Hendryx wrote prolifically during the thirties, appearing in most issues of *Short Stories*, and adding many hardbacks to the saga of the northwoods, such as "Man of the North" and "Blood of the North."

That same year (1917) the magazine went from a monthly to twice a month, which dropped the page count from 224 to 192. Later, due to a paper shortage, a nine-point type replaced the 10-point, and the pages shrank to 160, but with the same wordage, the editor assured his readers. This occurred in the September 3, 1920 issue. Not long after, the 10-point typeface came back. In October 1921, *Adventure* began coming out three times a month, 192 pages, and continued at this pace through 1925.

Another author who showed a great love for the Canadian wilds was William Byron Mowery, 23, and a hunter, trapper, university teacher at the time of his first story, in the September 10, 1923 issue. Not as productive in the pulps as Hendryx, Mowery would still come up with equally absorbing books later in career, such titles as "Heart of the North," and "Challenge of the North," both very romantic, and full of excitement.

Two western authors who appeared in *Adventure* near the beginning of their writing careers and went on to bigger and better things later were Ernest Haycox and Walter J. Coburn. Haycox's stories for the magazine were much more mature and well written than those appearing in *Western Story* some years later. Coburn had sold earlier, and had served in the air during the war. His father had discovered Last Chance

Gulch, where Helena now stands; like Tuttle, he could lay claim to a true western heritage. Haycox, of course, became famous for his mature westerns and at one time was the leading writer in the genre, and credited with elevating the pulp fiction to slick status, according to John A. Dinan, in *The Pulp Western.* Dinan notes that Coburn was the only pulp western writer with his name on two magazines: *Walt Coburn Western* and *Walt Coburn Action Novels.*

One of the writers, Edgar Young, asked a very appropriate question in "Camp-Fire" on one occasion: What is the spirit of adventure? Several readers responded by defining what to them the word meant. One thought it "is that curiosity that will not be satisfied without knowing from first-hand evidence what lies around the turn in the road and what lies behind the distant hill." Another felt a great amount of emotion in adventure. The most poetical description found the highest exemplification in a situation involving a boat stealing through the darkness, the oarlocks muffled, the moonlight filtering through the trees.

Another question that might have been asked, but wasn't, was, What is a hero? In *Adventure*'s case, it probably would be almost anyone but the typical stalwart, handsome figure found in romantic fiction. There was Hugh Pendexter's California Joe, a mountain and plains man; Clay Perry's "durable Dane," at the time the story opens, a battered, cadaverous has-been; Robert J. Horton's Coyote Jim, an old prospector astride his ancient mare, Bluebell; and F. St. Mars' various creatures that are the protagonists of his stories: cheetahs, peccaries, buffaloes, sloths.

As to be expected, Hoffman was very proud of his fiction package, as well he might be, considering the vast amount of time and effort he put into it. However, the fact that the magazine was printed on pulp paper bother him. He felt that many potential buyers of the magazine could be reached if they, too, overcame their prejudice against pulp paper fiction.

In a defense of his Writers' Brigade, he mentioned slick publications many contributed to, such as *Atlantic, Century,*

Collier's, *Saturday Evening Post* and *Scribner's*. He also named some of the outstanding scribes: Peter B. Kyne, Gouverneur Morris, Maurice Leblanc, Edgar Wallace, Albert Payson Terhune, Sir Rider Haggard, Octavus Roy Cohen, Warwick Deeping. Many of the magazine's stories ended up in book form. And editing these literary gems were members of the staff who were college graduates, even Rhodes Scholars and Phi Beta Kappas.

It was Hoffman's hope that somehow, his followers could spread the word about *Adventure*, and bring in many new readers, who would be eager to buy the magazine as soon as they knew about it. No indication is given as to how successful this actually turned out, but Hoffman did realize one of his dreams when, in late 1926, the October 23 issue came out with a better grade white paper and a new look in story headings and art. Within a year, pulp paper was back but by then Hoffman had moved on to a higher-class magazine.

For someone who had done graduate work in English, it's surprising to encounter so many misspelled words and faulty story constructions. Hoffman once explained the procedure for handling manuscripts. "Some of them were accepted after being read by only one of us, some read by two, three or even four, five, six or seven of us. . . . As each one reads, he makes a written note of every inconsistency, mistake or doubtful point that he finds. In the case of a long story one man may cover several pages with finely written notes and queries. . . . These notes and queries are sent to the author, who either shows that no change is necessary, or makes the changes, from the page numbers given, on a carbon copy of his manuscript, or indicates them to us by page number. Then one of us 'edits the copy' for the printer, seeing that these changes are properly embodied, making all typographical changes, conforming spelling to the Standard Dictionary ... and keeping his eye out for any mistakes the author and the rest of us have not caught."

Whew! Is this pulp writing and editing? Why, it almost sounds like a leisurely pastime for gentlemen who don't want to soil their cuffs. Where are the pulp hacks so much has been said about, who never had time to revise, so busy were they earning a penny a word? Where are the harried editors associated with pulp editorial offices, who don't even have time to read all copy once, much less make notes of inconsistencies? Apparently, *Adventure* functioned on another level, or perhaps pulp writing in the twenties was not the harried hurly-burly it became in the thirties.

But even though all evidence points to careful editing on the magazine, the fact remains that there was a consistency of misuse of certain phases and wrong spellings of certain words. Of course, without a 1920's edition of *Adventure*'s dictionary, one must rely on today's Webster's.

Hoffman certainly should have known better than to allow neither . . . or, which crops up repeatedly. He offset that mistake by allowing either . . . nor. In fact, he seemed just plain confused over the word nor. Sometimes it was no . . . nor. One of the stories had this sentence: "None of them wanted to gamble nor drink. . . ." He loved the phrase "under weigh," and used it repeatedly in all kinds of stories, even westerns, where the word "way" would have been more appropriate. The word "surprise" to him was always spelled "surprize." And he dropped the "u" in two words: "staunch," which came out "stanch," and "gauge," which appeared as "gage." In the latter case, it would be particularly misleading, since both are legitimate words, but with different meanings.

That these were Hoffman peccadilloes is evidenced by his words in "Camp-Fire"; undoubtedly the authors went along with him, since so few correctly spelled those particular words, which seemed to crop up continuously. In fact, a sort of repetitious permissiveness seemed to pervade many stories. Nothing in the way of one author necessarily copying ideas from another. But with so many stories dealing with the South Seas and Africa, it was inevitable that at some point in each the natives would be described and one author after another used the hackneyed phrase, "They were naked except for a breech cloth." It was never, "They only wore breech cloths. No, it was always, "They were naked except . . ."

This reached its redundancy in one story, when the description didn't stop with a simple wrap-around, but went on to tally up jewelry, coverings on legs, ornaments on the chest, until the poor native would have been so loaded down, he couldn't walk. But he was still "naked."

One other phrase that seemed to pop up over and over was, "Stranger in a Strange Land." Since Robert Heinlein hadn't written his book so titled at that time, it obviously was derived from the Bible. But hero after hero was such a stranger, and one western told in the first person had the protagonist explaining to everybody he was a "stranger in a strange land." So much for editorial foibles, in regard to word usages.

For Hoffman, women were a trial. The magazine had about 15 percent female readership, and Hoffman wasn't interested in any more. He gave short shrift to women letter writers when they complained that the magazine showed an aversion to their sex. He must have really sighed with exasperation, if not torn his hair, when a mother complained at the use of the word whore in a Gordon Young story. For years, the magazine had a quaint habit of using dashes for swear words. Even such innocuous a word as devil would not be printed. Sometimes, a page looked like a series of disjointed sentences, or pauses, with so many dashes. The woman's objection drew a two-page editorial from Hoffman, where he explained that a dash for an actual description would have been ridiculous. He did not see any threat to the morals of youngsters in using such a word; in fact, proper usage as in this case was a sane way to help instruct them in sex. His chagrin was probably mitigated by an earlier letter of praise, from a young woman. *Adventure* printed few such letters, but once in awhile one crept in. She said, "My first impulse in finishing each new copy . . . is to do as Old Misery did—leap in the air and crack my heels and give the scalp-yell. There are, perhaps, two reasons why I don't—an utter ignorance of the technique and the fact that I am a perfect lady and hesitate to prostrate the household. The second impulse, scarcely less strong, is to sit right down and tell you all about it.

"*Adventure* is the most thrilling, soul-satisfying magazine. It answers the desire, I think, everyone must have, if in varying degrees, for romance in its true sense—for something that stir's one blood and makes the eyes sparkle with joyous enthusiasm."

In the January 3, 1920 issue, the first "Off Trail" story was printed—an idea that sounded good but apparently didn't accomplish much. These were stories with an asterisk after them, to indicate that they were different from the usual run, or violated some canon of literature or custom of the magazine. The only trouble was, the fare was so varied to begin with that the epicurean would not realize he was savoring something different. The first "Off Trail" story was T.S. Stribling's "The Green Splotches." Interestingly enough, this may well have been the best "Off Trail" story the magazine would print, and it, at least, fulfilled the credo since science fiction did not appear in the magazine at all.

American scientists experience an unnerving situation. They come upon strange beings, looking like natives, but able to read men's minds. One of them, being told how chess is played, laughs at such a rudimentary game. It is soon clear that the entity has been stalking them in a human skin. Also, it has been determined that one of the men suffering from burns has been affected by radium. It's interesting to read the scientists' different explanations of what they think is happening as the story progresses—with further developments showing them their errors. The green splotches, incidentally, are from one of the other-world creatures who was wounded.

This story has been reprinted in various anthologies, one of them being *Famous Fantastic Mysteries* in 1952. In view of its high standing in science-fiction stories, it is worthwhile to hear what British author Gilbert Collins has to say about it. Collins himself appeared in *FFM*, with his "Valley of Eyes Unseen," and "The Starkenden Quest," both well received by the readers. In the December 1952 *FFM*, he writes:

"It is tantalizing indeed to have that spaceship whisked out of the reader's view almost as soon as glimpsed. That, I feel, is where the middle distance of the story ought to have started. Then, I am certain, Stribling, with his mastery in depicting the interplay of human character and motive, could have introduced plot and counterplot—a traitor in the explorers' midst, perhaps. . . . Where I must take off my hat to Stribling is at the passage where his amazingly accurate prophecies are made. They almost put him on the same plane with Wells, whom I take to be the supreme master of science fiction.

"I am also uneasy about Jupiter, too. No doubt Stribling used the giant planet with his eyes open, but the fact remains that to all with a layman's knowledge of astronomy, Jupiter will not do as a home of life. . . . But for long-shot accuracy of prediction, Stribling beats even Wells. . . . Compare his description of the appearance of his space ship as it sped homeward for Jupiter, with a hundred and one reports of the recent flying saucers, a weird luminosity outside the skin of the ship—but no external mechanism visible. His space ship standing on its tail is a master stroke, too. the admirable illustration of this might be a picture of one of the V-2 projectiles that, fired from Holland, hit London with such frightful accuracy and devastation only a few years ago."

Stribling would go on to win a Pulitzer Prize for later literary endeavors, and at that time, was winning the critics' approbation. "Fombombo" (August 20, 1923), derived from his visits to Central and South America in 1921, drew raves from Laurence Stallings, who said he hadn't "met with such excellent writing in a swash-buckling novel in many years." The London *Mercury* rated Stribling far above Ibanez (author of *The Four Horsemen of the Apocalypse*). Hoffman thought he would some day rank among the world's greatest satirists.

In fact, so infatuated was Hoffman, that he prefaced Stribling's "Web of the Sun" (January 30, 1922), an unusual practice, and quoted a critic who called the author on a rank with Voltaire and the greatest satirists of all times. The novel follows Charles Lassiter, a representative for a steamship company planning zeppelin passenger service in South America. He is accompanied on a trans-Andean junket by Exekiel Birdsong, an Arkansas missionary, who wants to sell Bibles. Birdsong often admonishes Lassiter for idolatry. They discovered a clustered society of natives in a crater, from which, they are told, there is no escape. Lassiter falls in love with Tilita. The story is reminiscent of Butler's "Erewhon," and like that one, somewhat static as it promulgates the natives' customs and beliefs. The satire seems mild, hardly a "rapier very deeply inserted in his notions of things in general," as the editor would have it.

There is, perhaps, more telling satire in Stribling's Poggioli series. A student of criminology through reading detective stories, Henry Poggioli is an American soap salesman in the Dutch West Indies who always arrives just as some crime has been committed. Before long, his fame precedes him, although it is clear that he never really quite understands just what is going on. He has definite ideas, but they often turn out wrong. The Poggioli stories have been collected in book form, but they hardly seem appealing to someone seeking mystifying detective fiction, since the protagonist is so inept.

The final story in the series appears in an issue after this study ends, but is appropriate to mention here. In "A Passage to Benares" (February 20, 1926), Poggioli encounters a mystery in a Hindu temple in Port of Spain, Trinidad. He is suspected of murdering a girl and thrown into jail. After much thought, Poggioli realizes who really perpetrated the crime, and calls the turnkey. Irate at finding that the murderer had been identified, he complains: "'What did you mean, keeping me locked up here when you knew I was an innocent man?'

"'Because I couldn't,' said the form with the lamp sorrowfully. 'Old Hira Dass didn't confess until a month or two after you were hanged, sir.'"

There were several authors in *Adventure* whose byline

readers saw month after month, who turned out a vast amount of material and were associated with one or more series. For air adventures, one needn't look any further than Thomson Burtis, a former newspaperman who covered Army camps during the war and served in the Air Service himself. He developed a whole group of likable pilots, serving out of McMullen Field, Texas, most of them prototypes of people Burtis knew. As he mentioned, when the series started everyone was alive. Then, one by one, the original pilots died or were killed. One of his most popular characters is Tex MacDowell, a typical daredevil who proves to be the best pilot at the field and who runs afoul of Dave Fitzpatrick, the most feared man on the border, and opium smuggler, among other illicit activities. "Feud's End" (February 28, 1922) is probably the best of the lot, in which Tex finally brings Fitzpatrick to account. The series was enjoyable but held few surprises.

Among the writers exploring the jungle, none found more hidden trails than Arthur O. Friel. In 1922, he took a trip up the Orinoco in Venezuela, but he had been writing about similar isolated South American regions for years. Many of his stories were told in the first person by a native, often Lucio Leon, known as Loco, a yellow-haired, blue-eyed Spaniard. Interesting background on Friel's stories was given here by Ted Baglin, and if doesn't mind my borrowing from him, I'll mention what he put together.

He reported that some of Friel's serials for *Adventure* were published in book form, and that five of the novels featured three recently mustered-out World War I veterans in the wilds of Venezuela. In one story they encounter Black White, "one of the most unusual continuing characters in pulp fiction," Baglin said. White had been a very handsome young man who gets involved with the daughter of the village chief. To prevent him from returning to civilization, she has a concoction prepared and administered in his drink which turns his skin repulsive. Being a vain man, he breaks down when he finds out what has happened to him, and now insane, leads a gang of plunderers. Later, he is restored to normalcy and returns to a new life.

In a change of pace, Friel tried his hand at an adventure set in the Catskills. This is one Baglin didn't mention. "Cat-o-'Mountain" (January 20, 1923) concerns vacationing newspaper man Douglas Hampton, and Marion Oaks, supposedly a daughter of "tainted" blood, since her father is Nigger Nat, but as in similar situations in such stories, only adopted and therefore unsullied and free to marry the hero. Mystery, a touch of supernaturalism, and plenty of good old mountain flavor set off this four-part serial. Friel notes that he himself once blundered into The Traps—the setting here—and like his protagonist Hampton, was accused of being a detective and ostracized by the community. A sequel involving some of the same characters was not as good.

Adventure's readers themselves must have been a hardy breed, beset as they were so continuously by wild natives, storms at sea, Mongol hordes, and pirate cutthroats, but always coming back for more. Perhaps some weakened after time, and felt like Berton Braley, in his poem "The Exile," in a 1924 issue:

> To eat without fear of infection
> To sleep without using a net,
> And throw away all my collection
> Of iodin, quinin et cet.
> To know all the noise and the clamor,
> The hurry and fret of the West
> I'd trade all the Orient glamour
> That damned lying poets suggest.

In checking *Adventure*'s tables of content, it is surprising to see that one of the biggest word producers of the pulps, namely H. Bedford-Jones, appears so infrequently. This would have been early in his career, so up to 1925 few Bedford-Jones stories appeared, although this writer later became a million-word-a-year man. Among his offerings were adventures about the swashbuckler Crawford and his strange quest, and the serial, "Rodomont," set in France in 1707, concerning two look-alikes, a mysterious prisoner at Mont St. Michel, and the usual Bedford-Jones swordplay and derring-do.

Probably the most series-minded of *Adventure*'s Writer's Brigade was Arthur D. Howden Smith. From a Cornish captain to a Norse sea rover, from an outlawed Jacobite in 18th century North America, to his son, kidnaped by pirates, he wrote convincingly and with great energy.

His Swain epics are typical: a strong-minded Norseman of the Orkneys, last outpost of his country's power, and his long and bloody feud with Frakork, the witch, and her bloodthirsty grandson, Olvir Rosta. There is no humor here; the hero is very inflexible and not likable, but very admirable. Eventually, Swain dies. Due to the popularity of the series, Smith brings him back by recounting earlier adventures that he devises to perpetuate the series.

A lighter approach was used in "The Doom Trail," a serial starting August 3, 1921, about Harry Ormerod, outlawed from England who comes to the new world and runs afoul of Black Death and Red Death, guardians of the gun runner's path through the forests. "Beyond the Sunset," a sequel, has Ormerod and his companions, as representatives of New York's governor, opening up land westward. His son, Robert, with Peter Corlaer, his father's comrade, and Pew and John Silver, are principals in *Porto Bello Gold*, a prequel to *Treasure Island*. And a great, great grandson of Robert is the hero of "A Manifest Destiny" (about William Walker) in a 1926 *Adventure*. And like so many of *Adventure*'s authors, Howden Smith utilized various historical sources for his works; he took many details from "The Orkneyinga Saga," a little-known chronicle of the Orkneys under the Norse *jarls* (rulers), for his Swain series. Since he was infringing on a beloved author's territory, he went to Robert Louis Stevenson's step-son and literary executor, Lloyd Osbourne, for whom *Treasure Island* was written, and asked if he minded a story borrowing characters and ideas from Stevenson's classic. Osbourne gave his blessing on the project. Smith built up some of the characters and tried to depict Silver, Bill Bones and others, as Stevenson had done. The story tells how Flint's pieces of eight came to be on Treasure Island, and Smith enjoyed writing it more than any other tale, he noted.

In 1924, Brentano's published a beautifully illustrated edition of *Porto Bello Gold* with H.C. Murphy, of the Artist's Brigade, doing the color plates. Murphy, however, was just one of many, many names associated with the magazine. In a typical year, some 15 to 20 different individuals would render covers, and an equal number for the inside black and white drawings. In 1923, a reader wrote that he wanted the covers to speak. From that time, "Camp-Fire" occasionally had one of the artists "rise and introduce himself." *Adventure*'s covers, while often rendered painstakingly, did not grab the newsstand browser as the more garish examples that came along later, on science fiction, detective, mystery and super hero pulps, would do. In the twenties, pulps did not promote a flamboyant approach, but in *Adventure*'s case, the covers continued as bland accompaniments even through the thirties. Such views as a polar bear rising in anger, a cowboy swinging a lariat, wolves howling, a mandarin scowling, an elk swimming, a pirate glowering, a volcano erupting—well, these were more like paintings that should hang in a studio; they had an impersonal feeling to them.

Unlike Howden Smith, who jumped from one century to another, and utilized written records for his stories, Leonard H. Nason laid claim only to the short time America fought in World War I, and his own experiences provided the impetus for the action. Nason served on a hospital ship, was with the M.P.s and the field artillery during the war, and was wounded in the Argonne; in fact, he nearly died. He was 27 when he sold his first story to *Adventure*, while working as an insurance claim adjuster. All the editors in the office, when the story arrived in February, 1922, enthusiastically embraced it—all, that is, but Hoffman who questioned its point of view and method of telling. The editor soon changed his mind, as Nason continued to supply the magazine exclusively with his output.

His style is elusive. He seems to be simply recounting the events, both ordinary and extraordinary, in a soldier's life. It's almost like a movie camera following the movements of its subject, with no attempt to edit for drama or suspense. That, perhaps, is the only drawback to Nason's method; he doesn't build to a climax. But his stories move so smoothly and logically, and read so effortlessly, they can truly be called works of art. Indeed, it wasn't long before he was receiving recognition. One reader commented: "You have certainly made a find in young Nason, as his stories are so natural as to be classed almost as facts." Laurence Stallings, who so admired T.S. Stribling, and who with Maxwell Anderson, wrote "What Price Glory," became equally enamored with Nason. "Mr. Nason's psychology is as good as his dialog and the soldier's outlook is reproduced with great fidelity."

Although he would write of doughboys trapped behind German lines, of soldiers hungry, tired, wet, cold, sick of fighting, wounded, lost, his attitude was not negative, and one doesn't have the feeling of futility encountered in such as "What Price Glory," or "All Quiet on the Western Front."

His descriptions were natural, and very visual, as shown in this example from "A Tragedy of Errors" (May 10, 1924). ". . . Eadie noticed a French soldier go to the long shed at one side of the square, where the farmers used to set up their stalls on market day, and bring out a hugh white star made of canvas that the sergeant had noticed standing against the wall . . .

"The French soldier carried the star into the center of the square and then laid it flat on the ground. Then he motioned all the bystanders to give way and leave a clear space. Eadie looked at all this in great wonder. He had a kind of hazy thought that the French soldier might be going to dance on the star or do some acrobatic stunt. No one seemed to be doing anything. They just stood and looked and left the star gleaming in white splendor.

"Then, as if someone had a string tied to their ears, everyone threw back his head and gazed aloft. Eadie did likewise. Far up, floating in the blue haze, was a plane. As Eadie watched it, it began to circle lower like a hawk over a hen yard. Down, down it came, until it was just above the roofs, when something was hurled out of it and the plane climbed into the upper altitude again. Whatever had been thrown out hurtled down and one could see a long streamer floating from it.

"Clank! It struck the ground. The French soldier stepped grandly out of the crowd, picked up the object, then, shouldering the star, he restored the latter to its place in the shed. Then he went off in the direction of corps headquarters."

His stories are replete with similar descriptions—interesting little sidelights that he seems to have an inexhaustible supply of.

If Nason covered all the battles and skirmishes of the war, down to the day-to-day affairs of the American soldier, then Hugh Pendexter told us everything else that ever happened in America up to that time.

The man was a walking historical encyclopedia. His method of preparing for a story was to get out 25 or books as reference, and weave together disparate facts, events and people. He was a compulsive writer, apparently. When he had a long serial to start in a particular issue, he would include a long letter to cite his sources and add additional background. The letters might go on for three pages or so. Hoffman regularly extolled Pendexter's virtues, explaining how he was bringing American history alive. So careful in his research was the author, that readers could not uncover an error in his writings. It was his intention, he said, to pick periods for his stories which were "a historical hinge on which our future development swung." Once, in answer to readers' requests for reference sources, he responded, "'I am enclosing a short list of books.'" The "short" list included 20 books on the early fur trade; two on early Santa Fe trade; some 15 on Indians in general; and some 27 on Indian tribes and religions.

As he said, "You can have a long a list as you care for." He had some 3,000 to choose from.

Unfortunately, in many of his stories, so relate with true-to-life details, you can't see the trappers for the trees. He seems to have downplayed the human angle to the point where the historical background holds the stage. Or else, he simply ignores the opportunity to develop a derring-do-type hero, even when the action seems to call for one.

In "Kings of the Missouri" (serial in August 3, 1920), the hero ostensibly is young Ralph Lander, but in reality the scout and trapper, Jim Bridger. In the serial "Rifle Rule" (May 10, 1924) first one young man, then a second, holds the stage, with neither emerging as the central character to grab the reader's interest.

Sometimes the "hero" is less than heroic, as in the serial "Gentlemen of the North" (November 3, 1919): "If he ever attacked me, I was determined not to cower like a sheep and be murdered, as I've known Chippewa squaws to die when their husbands were in a drunken fury."

One of his best accounts, which circumvents these inadequacies, if, indeed, that is what they are, heightens a lively chapter in the life of Daniel Boone. "When Kentucky Starved" (January 3, 1919) follows Boone and the hunter and trapper, Simon Kenton, as they stealthily slip through the Shawnee and Wyandot lines to upset the Indians' plans of capturing the fort. In his letter accompanying this 55-page novelette, Pendexter points out that "Boone was feared as a mighty destructive force, because home-makers always swarmed in his wake. But Kenton was a personal and malignant agency, an exasperating annoyance that enraged all the more for his audacity and seeming immunity. Once a prisoner there could be but one fate for him."

An idea of Pendexter's output is found in his production for 1922: six serials, either four or five parts each, plus the conclusion of a five-parter, and five short pieces on some aspect of history, not to mention the long letters, and an active correspondence he maintained with writers and readers.

An unusual development occurred in 1921, when the editors held an office discussion about surviving on a desert isle. The story would center on a group of men, without the usual wrecked ship nearby, or well-stocked boat. There would be no savages, no volcanoes, no rival parties, love interest, villains, buried treasure or handy items to use. It was agreed that J. Allan Dunn, who had written many sea stories, was the man for the job of bringing this group idea to life. As Hoffman said to Dunn: "'Let the men be ordinary, everyday types, such a bunch of chaps as you might pick coming up from the subway. Let the island not be one of those that extend a welcome at the very lip of the tide with convenient coconuts and self-sacrificing fish. Let them, with their everyday measures of knowledge, be up against the real thing from the start and work out their own salvation if they can.'"

Dunn goes on to explain how hard the story was to write. He put his "crusoes" in the stone age. Swimming from the place where they were wrecked to a better spot was an adventure in itself. Constructing a catamaran literally from scratch was an absorbing test of ingenuity, then sailing across the lagoon to an island and fighting off an attack by birds nesting there, tested their mettle further. He told how, without any implements ready-made, they constructed a house, built a fire, raised crops. It was a how-to primer on survival, told as if the author had been through the experience himself. The story was titled, "Barehanded Castaways," and appeared December 20.

Dunn received many letters on his unusual conception, with suggestions which he incorporated in the sequel, "The Island" (October 30, 1922). Brett, the leader of the group, remained on the island with a few others of the party, while the rest sailed away in a large catamaran to find civilization again and bring back provisions for those who had elected to make the island their home. There is a very absorbing and gripping situation that finds Brett trying to free one of the men whose foot is clamped in a clam. The sense of urgency mounts, as the man weakens from his long immersion in the water, his foot goes numb, the tides comes in, and Brett strains to keep him supported. "'There's the prof. He's on the porch. I think he's looking this way. He must see us. But it won't do any good. This is a _______ of a way to go, Brett! You'll stick as long as you can. . . .'" But Brett doesn't give up. He hangs on till the tide turns. Finally, he's able to pack into the clam's opening hot ashes and hot stones which cause the valve to open and thus frees his comrade.

If *Adventure* authors, who numbered in the hundreds, had for some reason stopped writing for one or two issues, the editor would have had to look no farther than Talbot Mundy to charge to the rescue. He was the most prolific of all, and could easily have filled single-handedly a month's worth of issues with his many creations: Ommony, Jimgrim, King, Ramsden, and his controversial Tros. "Camp-Fire" printed one of his letters three or four pages long, that answered someone's comments about the Egyptian pyramids. It included a diagram he drew—and all this from memory, since he didn't have his sources with him. What mattered that readers later wrote in to correct many of his statements? He had produced all that, with references to various authorities, from his capacious memory . . . and apparently, as effortlessly as someone else writing a letter of commendation. His stories are rich in the mystery of far-off places: India, the Orient, Tibet, peopled by heroic figures like Jimgrim, and foolish but likable camp-followers like Chullander Ghose, the exemplary and ferocious Narayan Singh, mystical leaders, fanatic religious followers, British officials both incompetent and efficient.

Mundy was born in London and came to the United States in 1911. His first appearance in *Adventure* was that year, with an article on pig-sticking in India. He traveled the world; he was laid low by cholera in Asia, stricken with black-water fever in German East Africa, and set upon by a gang in New York, resulting in a smashed-in jaw and broken skull. Through 1925, all but one of his stories found a home in *Adventure*, and nearly all were published in book form by the Bobbs Merrill Co. In 1917 he became an American citizen.

Mundy would tell how his character, Grim, was a real person, an American recruited by the British for intelligence work. In his stories, Mundy would feature one or two of his characters, then another one in a different story, then bring several together in another story. Thus, Athelstane King and Jeff Ramsden together are pitted against "The Gray Mahatma" (November 10, 1922), about a plot to overthrow the British rule in India, and one of two Mundy stories to be reprinted in *Famous Fantastic Mysteries* (the other being *Full Moon*). In another story, King and Ommony are together. Cottswold Ommony is a particularly appealing protagonist, with his rationalistic confidence and subtle ways of gaining his own ends, those being protection of India's forests. He often has to confound officialdom to achieve what he believes in. He is completely incorruptible, and sometimes a befriender of natives not in favor. In the six-part serial "Om" (October 10, 1924), he penetrates the mysterious and isolated Abor Valley. This and many of Mundy's other writings reflect his belief in mysticism, particularly transmigration. Mundy met Ommony's prototype in Bengal, during one of his trips there, and listened to his stories at night, about his love of the forests.

In 1925, Mundy started a series that evoked more comment, reader interest, suggestions, arguments—in fact, back and forth shouting—than anything ever printed in the magazine. This was the Tros presentation, "Tros of Samothrace" (February 10), the first of a long line of novels and novelettes about Caesar's invasion of Britain. Tros himself is cast somewhat in the mold of Swain, that is, inflexible in his ways, very strong, and a virile learner, but with more humor and less bloodthirstiness. He has a strange quirk. In a fight Tros thrusts two men into the sea, then berates his follower for killing the third.

"'But master, you killed two men!'

"'Not I. I gave them leave to swim,' said Tros.

"'They could not swim. They are all drowned, master."

"'That is their affair, I never forbade them to learn to swim!'

"'But that fellow in a bearskin—how could he have swum? His coat drowned him.'

"'He never asked my leave to wear that coat,' said Tros. 'I could have slain him with my sword as easily as you slew your man. But I spared him. I gave him leave to swim. No enemy of mine can hold me answerable for the bearskin coat he wears!'"

Now, after this specious reasoning, which Tros is sincere about, who can take such a hero seriously? Of course, many readers did, as this proved a very popular subject indeed. From it we might derive, "The noblest Roman of them all . . . was not Caesar." That seems to be Mundy's point in much of what he has to say.

"'I have followed Caesar's *Commentaries* as closely as possible in writing this story, but as Caesar, by his own showing, was a liar, a brute, a treacherous humbug and a conceited ass, as well as the ablest military expert in the field at that time, and as there is plenty of information from ancient British, Welsh and Irish sources to refute much of what he writes, I have not been to much trouble to make him out a hero." He says that Caesar, by his own confession, slew at least three million men and gave their women to be slaves. He goes on to further tarnish an image that has come down to us as representing an outstanding soldier, statesman, scholar. According to Mundy, the historians are at fault for copying from Caesar. He was an epileptic (a condition Mundy associated with vices) and addicted to all evils except drunkenness. In fact, he didn't even write his *Commentaries*, Mundy avers.

The response from readers came crackling back with the speed of bullets from a machine gun. "I think Mundy is a Grade A certified fiction writer but as an historical philosopher I think he is punk . . . ." "I think Mundy is full of pink prunes . . . ." A third found Caesar's licentiousness based on stories circulated by his political enemies. Hugh

Pendexter believed that General Lee would have run circles around Caesar's army, Stonewall Jackson would have whipped him on front and flanks, and Grant would have broken his neck.

Arthur Gilchrist Brodeur posed the most thoughtful disagreement. He couldn't find any place where Caesar "by his own showing," revealed himself a brute and a humbug, as Mundy contended. He went to Mundy's sources. He found no reason to believe Caesar didn't write the *Commentaries*; Cicero regarded them as Caesar's. And on the question of ancient British, Irish and Welsh sources, Brodeur found nothing in them about Caesar. Mundy answered many of his critics, but for some reason never replied in print to Brodeur, although a reader later comes to Mundy's defense in assailing Brodeur. The controversy continued to rage throughout 1925, with Mundy forceful enough himself to withstand such a long siege, but aided from time to time by others. No side seemed to gain a clear-cut advantage.

Without detracting from Mundy's recognized erudition, it might be pointed out that in talking to Wyatt Blassingame, a successful pulp writer of the thirties who knew Mundy, he revealed that on one occasion Mundy prefaced the chapters of a book of his with fake Latin quotations—a trick he said he used to give it more credence.

It was Blassingame, incidentally, who wrote to his brother, Lurton, a literary agent, of Mundy's death; he lived just a short distance from him at the time. Lurton forwarded the letter to *Adventure*, which was the first report the magazine had of his demise. Mundy died August 5, 1940, while in the midst of planning another junket through India. The November 1940 issue, which carried the obituary, reprinted Mundy's "The Soul of a Regiment." The story first appeared in 1912, was brought back by reader request in 1917 and 1935; it also was included in the 1926 book, *Adventure's Best Stories.* The only other printing equal in popularity was the Reverend Knickerbocker's sermon over the body of a gambler, Riley Grannan, which appeared four times.

With the passing of Mundy, we take leave of *Adventure*, much like saying goodbye to an old friend. But renewing acquaintances is easy. Just open the pages of any issue.

Stories of Life Love and
15¢
Adventure
JULY
1916
"BEYOND
THE RIM"
A Complete Novel
of the South Seas
by J Allan Dunn
"TO CRACK
A SAFE"
A Tale of
California
by Patrick &
Terence Casey
Stories by
H S Fullerton
F W Wallace
Robt V Carr
Henry Oyen
Thos Addison
H Liebe
Geo L Catton
W C Tuttle
D L Mackaye
and Others

PUBLISHED
TWICE A MONTH
Adventure

Adventure
F. C. HERBST

20th
25
THREE TIMES A MONTH
Adventure
W. C. Tuttle
Hugh Pendexter
George E. Holt
Talbot Mundy
Lynn Montross
Arthur M. Harris
Charles Victor Fischer
Douglas M. Dold

MAY
25c
PUBLISHED
THREE TIMES A MONTH
Adventure
J. Allan Dunn
George E. Holt
Hugh Pendexter
Charles Victor Fischer
F. R. Buckley
Charles Lee Bryson
William Wells

Adventure

AUGUST
8th
1926
25c
PUBLISHED
TWICE A MONTH
Adventure
Leonard H. Nason
Georges Surdez
Harold Lamb
Talbot Mundy
Gordon MacCreagh
Nevil Henshaw
Edmund M. Littell
Hamilton
3 Complete Novelettes

PUBLISHED
THREE TIMES A MONTH
Adventure
20th
25c
W. C. Tuttle
Nevil Henshaw
Hugh Pendexter
3 Complete Novelettes

FEBRUARY
10th
PUBLISHED
THREE TIMES A MONTH
Adventure
Hugh Pendexter
Ferdinand Berthoud
J. Allan Dunn
Ramon Stone Bradon
Gordon Young
Lloyd Kohler
F. St. Mars
F. J. Harroman

MAY
20th
1922
25¢
PUBLISHED
THREE TIMES A MONTH
Adventure
Bill Adams
Captain Dingle
W. C. Tuttle
Robert Simpson
Arthur Gilchrist Brodeur

Adventure
Gordon Young
Thomson Burtis
Orville Leonard
E. S. Pladwell
John T. Rowland
Brian Deever
Stanley Johnson
Townsend Boyer

Adventure

PUBLISHED
THREE TIMES A MONTH

Adventure

Frederick R. Bechdolt
Arthur D. Howden Smith
W. C. Tuttle
Hugh Pendexter
Albert Richard Wetjen
Joel Townsley Rogers
George F. Holt
Hubert Roussel
Chester L. Saxby
Oscar J. Friend

PUBLISHED
THREE TIMES A MONTH
Adventure
Georges Surdez
Harold Lamb
William P. Barron
Hugh Pendexter
Alan LeMay
Barry Scobee
Ralph R. Perry
Vance H. Morris
Leslie McFarlane
3 Complete Novelettes

APRIL
18th
1918
20¢
PUBLISHED
TWICE A MONTH
Adventure

PUBLISHED
TWICE A MONTH
Adventure

JULY
10th
1925
25c
PUBLISHED
THREE TIMES A MONTH
Adventure
Leonard H. Nason
L. Paul
Hugh Pendexter
Frederick Moore
Walter J. Coburn
Bill Adams
John Murray Reynolds
Fairfax Downey
Royce Brier
3 Complete Novelettes

FEBRUARY
3rd
1919
20¢
Adventure
PUBLISHED
TWICE A MONTH

PUBLISHED
THREE TIMES A MONTH
JUNE
30th
1922
25¢
Adventure
Frederick R. Bechdolt
Frank C. Robertson
Hugh Pendexter
L. Patrick Greene
F. St. Mars
Thomson Burtis
John Beames
Alan B. LeMay
A. Judson Hanna
Mary Gaunt

PUBLISHED
THREE TIMES A MONTH
MARCH
10th
1923
25¢
Adventure

Bill Adams
J. D. Newsom
Georges Surdez
Albert Richard Wetjen
Hugh Pendexter
Barry Scobee
George Bruce Marquis
William Wells

Adventure

PUBLISHED
THREE TIMES A MONTH
E. S. Pladwell
George E. Holt
Novelettes

Adventure

Adventure
Leonard H. Nason
Georges Surdez
Albert Richard Wetjen
Dingle
H. Bedford-Jones
Edmund M. Littell
Andrew A. Caffrey
Novelettes

Adventure

MARCH
PUBLISHED
TWICE A MONTH
25¢
Adventure
John L. Cochrane
Talbot Mundy
Ferdinand Berthoud
John Buchan
Thomson Burtis
Arthur O. Friel
Walter Mills
W. C. Tuttle
Romaine H. Lowdermilk
W. Townend
Harrison R. Howard
Konrad Bercovici

TWICE A MONTH
Adventure

Adventure
Complete Novel

Adventure

PUBLISHED
TWICE A MONTH
Adventure

PUBLISHED
THREE TIMES A MONTH
APRIL
10th
1922
25¢
Adventure

Our Camp-Fire came into being May 5, 1912, with our June issue, and since then its fire has never died down. Many have gathered about it and they are of all classes and degrees, high and low, rich and poor, adventurers and stay-at-homes, and from all parts of the earth. Some whose voices we used to know have taken the Long Trail and are heard no more, but they are still memories among us, and new voices are heard, and welcomed.

We are drawn together by a common liking for the strong, clean things of out-of-doors, for word from the earth's far places, for man in action instead of caged by circumstance. The *spirit* of adventure lives in all men; the rest is chance.

But something besides a common interest holds us together. Somehow a real comradeship has grown up among us. Men can not thus meet and talk together without growing into friendlier relations; many a time does one of us come to the rest for facts and guidance; many a close personal friendship has our Camp-Fire built up between two men who had never met; often has it proved an open sesame between strangers in a far land.

Perhaps our Camp-Fire is even a little more. Perhaps it is a bit of leaven working gently among those of different station toward the fuller and more human understanding and sympathy that will some day bring to man the real democracy and brotherhood he seeks. Few indeed are the agencies that bring together on a friendly footing so many and such great extremes as here. And we are numbered by the hundred thousand now.

If you are come to our Camp-Fire for the first time and find you like the things we like, join us and find yourself very welcome. There is no obligation except ordinary manliness, no forms or ceremonies, no dues, no officers, no anything except men and women gathered for interest and friendliness. Your desire to join makes you a member.

AN INTERESTING contribution to the discussion on the use of tobacco among the Cossacks:

Nuevo Laredo, Mexico.

Just a line or two regarding the discussion of tobacco in the issue of May 20, 1924, with particular reference to its use among the Cossacks:

LAMB'S observation that the Cossacks might have had the tobacco introduced to them by the Spaniards *via* Constantinople and the Turks seems based on his statement that the English trade with Russia through the Baltic was negligible in 1630 (the approximate time of the Czar's ban against the use of tobacco). The real explanation is that tobacco was introduced to the Russians through an English trading-post established at Archangel on the White Sea. The White Sea had been discovered in the time of the Tudors (the Tudor reign ended with Elizabeth in 1603) and a Russian Company was formed for the purpose of establishing and conducting the Archangel post. Yearly fairs were held there where Jamaica sugar, pepper, knives, etc., were traded for hemp, tallow and the "roe of the sturgeon of the Volga," according to Macaulay. But, continues Macaulay, "there was a secret traffic"—tobacco. Cow's horns, perforated, served the Muscovite for a pipe. "Every Archangel fair . . . best "Virginia rolls," "speedily found their way to Novgorod and Tobolsk."

There is the cycle complete—the roe of the sturgeon of the Cossack country for "Virginia rolls." The Czar's ukase, it would appear, was designed more to wipe out a strange new vice (?) than to dislodge a custom. Since tobacco was under extensive cultivation long before James I died (1625) it would readily appear that the tobacco had been introduced to the Volga country through Archangel, possibly as much as 10 years before the Czar's proscription of 1630.—H. L. W.

TOM L. MILLS of our A. A. staff, sends a coo-ee across to Camp-Fire from New Zealand and hands us an Australian newspaper clipping setting forth a large snake-story. The Albury district, he explains, is on the border between Victoria and New South Wales.

A snake story, which is remarkable even among stories of that class being featured in the Press. A youth named Clifford Scholes, residing in the Albury district has been in hospital five times during the past few weeks for treatment for snake bites. The remarkable features of the case are that since the fourth bite he has been carefully guarded by another boy to prevent the snakes from attacking him, and that the snakes have not been seen by other people. Scholes himself declares that they

A Free Question and Answer Service Bureau of Information on Outdoor Life and Activities Everywhere and Upon the Various Commodities Required Therein. Conducted for *Adventure* Magazine by Our Staff of Experts.

QUESTIONS should be sent, not to this office, but direct to the expert in charge of the section in whose field it falls. So that service may be as prompt as possible, he will answer you by mail direct. But he will also send to us a copy of each question and answer, and from these we shall select those of most general interest and publish them each issue in this department, thus making it itself an exceedingly valuable standing source of practical information. Unless otherwise requested inquirer's name and town are printed with question; street numbers not given.

When you ask for *general* information on a given district or subject the expert may give you some valuable general pointers and refer you to books or to local or special sources of information.

Our experts will in all cases answer to the best of their ability, using their own discretion in all matters pertaining to their sections, subject only to our general rules for "Ask Adventure," but neither they nor the magazine assumes any responsibility beyond the moral one of trying to do the best that is possible. These experts have been chosen by us not only for their knowledge and experience but with an eye to their integrity and reliability. We have emphatically assured each of them that his advice or information is not to be affected in any way by whether a given commodity is or is not advertised in this magazine.

1. **Service free to anybody, provided self-addressed envelop and *full* postage, *not attached*, are enclosed. (See footnote at bottom of page.) Correspondents writing to or from foreign countries will please enclose International Reply Coupons, purchasable at any post-office, and exchangeable for stamps of any country in the International Postal Union.**
2. **Send each question direct to the expert in charge of the particular section whose field covers it. He will reply by mail. Do NOT send questions to this magazine.**
3. **No reply will be made to requests for partners, for financial backing, or for chances to join expeditions. "Ask Adventure" covers business and work opportunities, but only if they are outdoor activities, and only in the way of general data and advice. It is in no sense an employment bureau.**
4. **Make your questions definite and specific. State exactly your wants, qualification and intentions. Explain your case sufficiently to guide the expert you question.**
5. **Send no question until you have read very carefully the exact ground covered by the particular expert in whose section it seems to belong.**

1. The Sea Part 1 American Waters
BERIAH BROWN, 1624 Biegelow Ave., Olympia, Wash. Ships, seamen and shipping; nautical history, seamanship, navigation, yachting, small-boat sailing; commercial fisheries of North America; marine bibliography of U. S.; fishing-vessels of the North Atlantic and Pacific banks. (*See next section.*)

2. The Sea Part 2 British Waters
CAPTAIN A. E. DINGLE, care *Adventure*. Seamanship, navigation, old-time sailorizing, ocean-cruising, etc. Questions on the sea, ships and men local to the British Empire go to Captain Dingle, not Mr. Brown.

3. The Sea Part 3 Statistics of American Shipping
HARRY E. RIESEBERG, Apt. 347-A, Kew Gardens, Washington, D. C. Historical records, tonnages, names and former names, dimensions, services, power, class, rig, builders, present and past ownerships, signals, etc., of all vessels of the American Merchant Marine and Government vessels in existence over five gross tons in the United States, Panama and the Philippines, and the furnishing of information and records of vessels under American registry as far back as 1760.

4. Islands and Coasts Part 1 Islands of Indian and Atlantic Oceans; the Mediterranean; Cape Horn and Magellan Straits
CAPTAIN A. E. DINGLE, care *Adventure*. Ports, trade, peoples, travel. (*See next section.*)

5. Islands Part 2 Haiti, Santo Domingo, Porto Rico, Virgin and Jamaica Groups
CHARLES BELL EMERSON, Adventure Cabin, Los Gatos, Calif. Languages, mining, minerals, fishing, sugar, fruit and tobacco production.

6. ★ New Zealand; and the South Sea Islands Part 1 Cook Islands, Samoa
TOM L. MILLS, *The Feilding Star*, Feilding, New Zealand. Travel, history, customs; adventure, exploring, sport. (*Postage two cents.*)

7. South Sea Islands Part 2 French Oceania (Tahiti, the Society, Paumoto, Marquesas); Islands of Western Pacific (Solomons, New Hebrides, Fiji, Tonga); of Central Pacific (Guam, Ladrone, Pelew, Caroline, Marshall, Gilbert, Ellice); of the Detached (Wallis, Penrhyn, Danger, Easter, Rotuma, Futuna, Pitcairn).
CHARLES BROWN, JR., P. O. Box 308, San Francisco, Calif. Inhabitants, history, travel, sports, equipment, climate, living conditions, commerce, pearling, vanilla and coconut culture.

8. ★ Australia and Tasmania
PHILLIP NORMAN, 842 Military Rd., Mosman, Sydney, N. S. W., Australia. Customs, resources, travel, hunting, sports, history. (*Postage ten cents.*)

9. Malaysia, Sumatra and Java
FAY-COOPER COLE, Ph. D., Field Museum of Natural History, Chicago, Ill. Hunting and fishing, exploring, commerce, inhabitants, history, institutions.

10. ★ New Guinea
L. P. B. ARMIT, Port Moresby, Territory of Papua, *via* Sydney, Australia. Hunting and fishing, exploring, commerce, inhabitants, history, institutions. Questions regarding the measures or policy of the Government or proceedings of Government officers not answered. (*Postage ten cents*).

11. Philippine Islands.
BUCK CONNOR, L. B. 4, Quartzsite, Ariz. History, inhabitants, topography, customs, travel, hunting, fishing, minerals, agriculture, commerce.

12. Hawaiian Islands and China
F. J. HALTON, 1402 Lytton Bldg., Chicago, Ill. Customs, travel, natural history, resources, agriculture, fishing, hunting.

13. Japan
GRACE P. T. KNUDSON, Castine, Me. Commerce, politics, people, customs, history, geography, travel, agriculture, art, curios.

★ ***(Enclose addressed envelop with ten cents in stamps NOT attached)***

Bait and Fly Casting for Bass

HOW to vary your lure according to the weather:

Question:—"I would like full information on fresh-water fishing, principally in Virginia. I love to fish but have never had a chance until this Summer to take a real trip nor to study the finer points which I am sure it takes, covering tackle and equipment, fly and bait-casting bait to use, camping-outfit and trips. Principal fishing of this community is bass, yellow and spotted suckers, perch, etc."—C. RICHARD BOYCE, Winchester, Va.

Answer, by Mr. Thompson:—Doubtless you will want to do both bait and fly-casting for your bass. The bait-casting outfit requires a rod about five feet long with reel-seat above hand-grasp. The fly rod should be nine or nine and one-third feet long with reel-seat below hand. The bait-casting rod is to be equipped with a quadruple multiplying reel, and braided silk line of about fourteen-pound test. You can use almost any kind of bait-casting lures, as bass strike at them avidly; these include the wooden minnows or wabblers and all kinds of spoons and spinners. I am enclosing a little booklet on bait-casting which I know will help you master the art.

In fly-fishing you use an enameled line that balances the rod and then attach a gut leader and your flies. There are numbers of patterns, and the best suggestion in using them is: On bright days dark flies, on cloudy days bright flies. This does not always work out. The smaller flies on hooks from four to ten are very good for perch. In fly-fishing you use either a single-action ordinary or automatic reel.

For sucker-fishing mostly worms are used as bait.

Please write me again about what kind of camping you intend to do, whether going alone or with a party and for how long, and I shall immediately answer. When I am provided with this information I can inform you better. Also whether you are going to take a car or not.

Gorillas

ALSO a few words about another animal, the most dangerous of all those that roam the veld:

Question:—"According to the lists in *Adventure* I believe you are the one I should write to in regard to the savage gorilla.

I would prefer to hear the opinion of hunters rather than official reports as to their temper. Will they attack in defense of dead young?

Would you tell a story or two about them to show cunning or lack of it?

The most dangerous beast or reptile, in your section?"—H. G. REPPETOE, Maumee, O.

Answer, by Capt. Franklin:—About the only time a gorilla will attack is in defense of its young. They are then extremely dangerous. A gorilla is so powerful that he makes short work of a man if he gets hold of him, usually tearing his windpipe out.

Gorillas are very cunning. They throw sentries out during the daytime; these sentries are relieved at regular intervals with clock-like precision, and I have seen huge boulders worn as smooth as a piece of glass and polished as if by varnish from the continual tread of these sentries on the same boulder.

The most dangerous beast in my section is the buffalo. These animals, unlike a lion, which usually slinks away, will attack you as soon as they wind you.

I would advise you to buy F. C. Selous' book on "Big Game Hunting in Africa."

LOST TRAILS

NOTE—We offer this department of the "Camp-Fire" free of charge to those of our readers who wish to get in touch again with old friends or acquaintances from whom the years have separated them. For the benefit of the friend you seek, *give your own name if possible*. All inquiries along this line, unless containing contrary instructions, will be considered as intended for publication in full with inquirer's name, in this department, at our discretion. We reserve the right in case inquirer refuses his name, to substitute any numbers or other names, to reject any item that seems to us unsuitable, and to use our discretion in all matters pertaining to this department. Give also your own full address. We will, however, forward mail through this office, assuming no responsibility therefor. We have arranged with the Montreal *Star* to give additional publication in their "Missing Relative Column," weekly and daily editions, to any of our inquiries for persons last heard of in Canada. Except in case of relatives, inquiries from one sex to the other are barred.

McDERMOTT, W. Resident of Texas. Formerly of U. S. S. *St. Louis* and U. S. S. *McLeash*, U. S. N. Last heard from he was bound for Denver, Colo. Write to your Pard and Double.—Address THE DUTCHMAN.

MITCHELL, ETTA and Laura. Sisters of T. W. Mitchell of Fargo, N. D. Last heard from in Washington or Oregon in 1916. Any information will be appreciated by their nephew.—Address GORDON MITCHELL, 898 Caldwell Ave., Bronx, N. Y. C.

A COMPLETE list of unclaimed mail will be published in December 30th and June 30th issues of Adventure.

MORGAN, WALTER V. Please write your old Pal.—Address HARLEY E. ROGERS, care of S. C. E. Co., Big Creek, Calif.

BATEMAN, LEONARD. Formerly a resident of Baltimore, Md., and also Minneapolis. Last heard of in Minneapolis in 1915. Supposed to have gone West. Important news and funds.—Address C. E. BATEMAN, Minneapolis, Minn.

GREEN, JOHN. Last heard from when he was discharged from Camp Dodge, Sioux Falls, South Dakota. Any information will be appreciated.—Address PATRICK CANEY, 713 East Long Ave., New Castle, Pa.

CURTS, FRANK E. Theatrical name Frank Manning. Disappeared from Lusk, Wyoming, about March, 1918, while engaged in business of quarrying. For years prior thereto he had conducted the Frank Manning Shows. Height five feet six inches, light hair, blue eyes, solid build, scar over left eye on the forehead. Any information will be appreciated.—Address R. M. ANDERSON, Beloit, Kansas.

MITCHELL, DR. GORDON. Son of a sister of Thomas Wesley Mitchell. Age about thirty-five or forty-five years. Has a sister by the name Claudia. Last name unknown. Any information will be appreciated.—Address THOMAS GORDON MITCHELL, 898 Caldwell Ave., Bronx, N. Y. C.

TOMB, WILLIAM. Last heard of he was in Denver, Colo., in January, 1922. Have good news for him.—Address EDWARD TRUETER, R. R. 2., Bonner Springs, Kansas.

THOMPSON, MYRON and Lawrence. Ages twenty and nineteen respectively. Last heard from several years ago in Milwaukee, Wis. Any information will be greatly appreciated.—Address F. HAMILTON, Box 1326, East Chi, Indiana.

EADON, LIONEL ALFRED. Age fifty-three. Prospector, born in London, Eng. Blue eyes. Last seen five years ago in Nevada City, Calif. Worked for the Delhi Mining Co., Nevada, Calif., in 1918. Missing for twenty-one years. Any information will be appreciated by his mother and sister.—Address MRS. M. VALENCIA, 317 S. Grant St., Stockton, Calif.

BARR, JOSEPH L. Served in Co. A, 6th U. S. Inf. on Panay, P. I., 1900 to 1902. Any information will be appreciated.—Address F. G. CARR, 723 Gough St., San Francisco, Calif.

BROTHEN, CARL or Charley. Last heard from in Spokane, Wash. Has a homestead in Lovejoy, Montana. Age thirty-three years, height five feet ten inches, weight one hundred and sixty pounds, brown hair and blue eyes. Any information will be appreciated by his mother and brother.—Address LOUIS BROOTEN, Alessa Lake, B. C., Canada.

THE following have been inquired for in either the June 30 or July 30, 1924 issues of Adventure. They can get the name and address of the inquirer from this magazine:

ADAMS, Joe; Bowman, Jesse; Clarence, Roy P.; Coghlan, C. C. Conniston, Art; Connors, Eugene, or Gene (Chuck); Cook, Harvey Lawrence; Dillmore, Jack; Dohl, Frank; Durning, Frank; Fleisch, Florence; Gordon, Frank; Hines, Hugh W.; Hollis, Clarence C.; Holland, James Arthur; Keith, Henry; Kelly, John H.; Little, Thomas; Mann, Herbert, Jr.; Morgan, Newton, A.; Parrish, Harry; Reed, Claud; Tillman, Albert; Van Marter, Frank E.

MISCELLANEOUS—Brother and two sisters of Miss Josephine Thompson; Case family; relatives of Hazel Chreiman; "Snake Eye Scotty"; Troop K, Fifth Cavalry. Members Petry, Kelly, Thompson, G. O. or any others that were in Mexico in 1919; U. S. S. *Chicago* Members of her crew from April 6, 1917 while in "Rio" and Southern American ports; Women members of Camp-Fire please write to me; Z. T. H.

THE TRAIL AHEAD

AUGUST 20TH ISSUE

Besides the **complete novel** and the **complete novelette** mentioned on the second contents page of this issue, the next *Adventure* will bring you the following stories:

THE CAPTIVE — *George E. Holt*
Diplomacy and kidnaping in Morocco.

A RIMROCK JUDAS — *Alex. McLaren*
"*Shorty*" knew there was gold beneath the basalt.

X-35, CHARGÉ D'AFFAIRES — *Gerald C. Huntoon*
The submarine commander has a bright idea.

IROQUOIS! IROQUOIS! A Five-Part Story Part II — *Hugh Pendexter*
The half-breed, *Gentry*, shows his colors.

SIR MELLIVORA — *Leo Walmsley*
Braver than a lion.

SERVANTS OF THE LAW — *H. Mortimer Batten*
Nahora could not fathom the white man's code.

DJONGOS — *John Scarry*
He was an ape—his master was murdered.

Still Farther Ahead

THE three issues following the next will contain long stories by Leonard H. Nason, E. S. Pladwell, Joel Townsley Rogers, F. R. Buckley, Hugh Pendexter, W. C. Tuttle, William Byron Mowery, Frederick Moore, Arthur D. Howden Smith and Georges Surdez; and short stories by J. D. Newsom, H. C. Bailey, Clements Ripley, Leo Walmsley, John Webb, Douglas Oliver, Dale Collins, F. St. Mars, H. C. Wire, J. Allan Dunn and others; stories of Naval aviation, pearlers in the South Seas, York Staters in Indian days, cattle-rustlers on the Western range, viking-farers in Norwegian fiords, gobs in Central American waters, French troopers in Africa, knights-at-arms in the Middle Ages, adventurers the world around.

INDEX

www.ingramcontent.com/pod-product-compliance
Lightning Source LLC
LaVergne TN
LVHW091205080426
835509LV00006B/841

* 9 7 8 1 4 3 4 4 9 6 1 7 1 *